Table of Contents

Dedications

To the sports tourism and events leaders that strive to make a difference. We hope this book meets the high standards that you set for our industry every day.

To the mentors that preceded us.
Coach Learing, Dr. Baker, Jack Kelly, Kevin Gray, Jack Hughes, Sherm Miller, my Dad Rich.
I hope you are looking down on us with a smile.
I hope I can give to others as much as you gave to me.

To those that wear the "backpacks," this book is for you.

Introduction

"Champions are made from something they have deep inside them....a desire, a dream, a vision."
– Muhammad Ali

"Become a Leadership CHAMPion"

There are thousands of commentaries about the core traits that define a great leader. Theories abound on what makes one person a leader, and another a follower. As sports industry professionals, we are all accountable as leaders in one way or another. We lead work teams, Local Organizing Committees (LOCs), volunteers, boards, staff members, interns, and our organizations as a whole. As a leader, we must always be sharpening our skills in preparation for the next big challenge.

In our work with our various clients, we are often asked to evaluate the organization's environment, both internally and externally. This process often uncovers the rock star team members, the ones who are truly leading the effort day in and day out – the Champions of the organization. These talented individuals come in many shapes and sizes, however, most great leaders we find embody five key characteristics that make them a leadership CHAMPion....

Collaborator – George W. Bush once said, "A leader is someone who brings people together." The ability to work with others and build working teams is a vital tool for all great leaders. At the Huddle Up Group, we believe this is the single most important trait of successful people (and companies). You can't always do it on your own; you need others to participate to reach your long-term goals. The ability to collaborate is critical to that end.

Humility – One of the most difficult things to do is to stand back and give credit to others. After all, we work in sports, where competition is part of the job. We all want to "win" and personal acclimation comes with success. The best leaders are those who not only can easily attribute victory to the team as a whole, but they can also take the blame when things go poorly (even if it wasn't their fault). By their nature, humble people are well equipped to garner buy-in, and lead organizations to prosperity. They make it about the team and not the individual, creating an atmosphere rich in partnership and teamwork, which in the end leads to high achievement.

Action-oriented – The top people in any field are not afraid to take action. Of course, some leaders take longer to map out their game plans, but once the goals are identified, leaders aggressively launch into action. For leaders, mistakes are simply part of the process, so there is no fear of activating an initiative.

Mentorship – Leaders think about the long-term, not just tomorrow. In order to have sustainable success, leaders must not only continually improve their own performance, but also grow the skills of those around them. Mentorship, for both the leader and the follower, is critical to continually raise the bar. We find that the cream of the crop in our industry make time not only to mentor their followers, but also to be mentored by others.

Preparation – Alexander Graham Bell, Abraham Lincoln, Colin Powell, Arthur Ashe....These men all cite preparation as the most important key to success. Great leaders not only prepare, but they often over-prepare. That is, they go to extreme measures to know everything about a situation. For instance, in a bid process your preparation may include: determining the decision makers (a person or a committee?), what are their major event priorities (venue condition or volunteer management?), what is the financial agreement for the championship (bid fee or venue rental assistance, shared P/L?), and what can we add that will make the event the best of its kind (athlete and official hospitality?). There is a saying that lawyers use when talking about trying a case in court: "Don't ever ask a question that you don't already know the answer to." To a certain extent, this is also true in the sports tourism and events industry. We should never go into a meeting or a planning process without having all the information we need to achieve success. For great leaders, preparation is every bit as important as execution.

Collaborate, be humble, take action, mentor and be mentored, and prepare for success. No matter your position in the sports tourism and events industry, these are the elements that will lead to sustained success. These five characteristics combine to make leaders into CHAMPions.

So, you may ask, why do we open a book about service with a commentary about leadership? Simple. Leadership is the core tenant to success not only in sports tourism, but in life. The tenets laid out above apply to every chapter of this book. Whether you are a leader or a follower, in whatever situation presents itself, impeccable service demands that the five CHAMPion characteristics be present. With that in mind, we hope you enjoy the book.

<u>Author's Note</u>: *Sports Service* is laid out in a seven-stage linear format. The book begins with bidding on events, weaves through the execution elements of the event, and ends with post-event follow-up tactics. In each stage there are three best practice takeaways for three different industry segments:

(1) Host destinations (sports commissions, CVBs, LOCs, venue managers),

(2) Event rights holders (NGBs and event owners),

(3) Hospitality leaders (host hotels, restaurants, attractions).

At the end of each stage there are discussion questions, and where appropriate, case studies on that stage's subject matter. Finally, there is a complimentary test that accompanies this book and can be administered as part of a "Sports Service Professional (SSP)" training for host destinations upon request. Contact the author for more details on the SSP program.

Stage I
Event Bidding for Success

Event rights holders make buying decisions every day. They buy destinations, tournament venues, hotels, and host organizations (such as a CVB or sports commission). There are more choices for these event owners today than ever before. The competition for the sports tourism industry's top events is at an all-time high, and the venue arms race in the industry has achieved record levels.

So how does a destination cut through the clutter and differentiate itself against its peers? Service.

Unilaterally, the top host destinations in the sports events industry are great at supporting their clients (the event rights holders). Generally speaking, the best host communities handle everything outside the lines so their clients can concentrate on delivering a superior championship experience for their athletes, families, and fans (by focusing their energy inside the lines).

You may ask, "So what does being a good host have to do with the bid process?" Excellent question. In the end, if you cannot determine what the needs of the client are in advance (such as during the bid process), then the ultimate success of your bid is already compromised.

For the purpose of this program, *Sports Service*, we surveyed some of the top industry professionals on a myriad of topics. We not only sought the opinion of event rights holders, but also of the top host organizations, venue managers, team travel coordinators, third parties, host hotels, athletes, and coaches. Our goal was to provide a well-rounded view of what each side of the industry is looking for to be able to best service sports groups. What we found was not surprising: what is important to one side of the market may not be a top priority of another. That said, to be successful, each industry participant must at least understand the priorities of the others in the equation. That is what this program sets out to help you with.

So, back to the question at hand: "What does being a good host have to do with the bid process?" We will answer that question with a series of questions....

If you are a host community or hotel, do you know what the three most important things are to the event rights holders we surveyed? The top three, in order are:

1. Community engagement and volunteerism – Rights holders need qualified and engaged volunteers to help execute their event. The communities that deliver in this area are likely to be at the top of their list the next time that a rights holder chooses a host site.

2. Ease of access to the market – If you don't have a major airport, and great drivability, your destination will likely have to overcome this in the bid process.

3. Local hospitality – An ample supply of restaurants, bars, and attractions are important to event rights holders. Keeping teams and their families busy during down times takes the pressure off of the tournament organizer so they can focus on the next round of competition.

Notice the top three items for event professionals didn't include anything about hotels. Perspective on what is important is key, and nowhere is that more important than the bid process.

Same question, different group. If you are an event organizer, what do you believe are the three most important things to the host community? Here they are:

1. Communication – This applies to not only the rights holder and host relationship, but also to the local clubs or teams that may be party to the tournament. Many host cities feel like they are drawn in to plug communication gaps between a host club and their sanctioning body running the event. Also, many host organizations

surveyed felt that the level of communication, and the timeliness of it (coming too late in the game from the event owner), was a challenge. The rule of thumb should be to communicate early and often.

2. Third-party housing issues – Not the kind you would think. Several survey respondents cited the over-involvement of third-party housing companies in the actual event itself, which often causes logistical issues. Very few housing companies have extensive event execution experience, so ask them to stay in their lane and handle housing, nothing more. Role clarity here is key.

3. Reporting – CVBs and sports commissions are often asked to provide financial incentives to event rights holders in the form of bid fees or other support. More and more, the boards that govern these host organizations are looking for some form of ROI reporting on what those incentive-type funds generated. That can be room nights, economic impact, or another matrix of some kind. In the end, the host needs the help of the rights holder to gather relevant data to support their investment in your event. Challenges in gathering reporting data was cited on numerous surveys for this project. The host agencies act in good faith when they supply

these incentives, so it's only fair to ask the event rights holder to return the favor post-event.

So now that we have looked at how one side of the bargaining table may have a different view of success than the other, how can we bridge the gap to garner win-win partnerships? The following is a case study on how to do just that.

Case Study: Creative Event Bidding

"You have to learn the rules of the game, and then you have to play better than anyone else."
– Albert Einstein

"Game Changer"

One of the great fictional characters of all time, Captain James Tiberius Kirk of the Starship Enterprise, hated losing so much he actually changed the rules of the game. For *Star Trek* fans, you will remember the tale of the "Kobayashi Maru, No-Win Scenario." In the television show and later in the movie series, the Kobayashi Maru was a training exercise for future leaders of star fleet command. The flight simulator used in the exercise is programmed by a computer to offer the captain (in this case Kirk) zero possible outcomes of success. Basically,

---

the ship crashes and the crew die no matter what the captain does, thusly a "no-win scenario" (the Maru was so popular with *Star Trek* fans it even has its own Wikipedia page).

Our fearless Captain Kirk, having failed the test on numerous occasions, became the first and only person to ever defeat the Kobayashi Maru. On the eve of the exam, Kirk changed the program to offer a winning outcome. While he was reprimanded for essentially cheating on the test, he was also commended for creative thinking. Kirk changed the game.

As sports industry professionals, we rarely encounter "no-win scenarios", but we can still learn from William Shatner's character. We must always look for winning opportunities to change the playing field and slant the outcome in the favor of our destinations. Here is one real-life example that achieved a game-changing outcome.

In 1999, the Western Athletic Conference (WAC) had 16 teams and was the country's first collegiate "super conference." That year, a core group of members from the WAC left to start their own league, now known as the Mountain West Conference. The departure of these members presented some challenges for the WAC, and an opportunity for our sports commission in Tulsa.

The University of Nevada Las Vegas (UNLV) was part of the group that left for the new conference. UNLV at the time was the long-running host of the WAC Basketball Championship. Essentially, with its departure, the history of the event – its sponsor support and the arena it was played in – moved to the new Mountain West Conference along with UNLV. The WAC had to find a new home for their marquee event and replace the financial loss of its title sponsor.

The WAC issued an RFP to all of its members, including the University of Tulsa. The RFP was for two years. Seven schools, some with their DMOs and sports commissions, put forth bids. Our bid in Tulsa, with the University and the Sports Commission as partners, was very unique in three ways.

One, we brought a title sponsor to the table as part of our bid. If the tournament was played in Tulsa, the title sponsor would commit cash and other resources to support the event. We solved one of the WAC's major problems, and in essence, changed the game.

Second, our title sponsor put terms in the agreement that the tournament would need to be in Tulsa for three years rather than the two that were in the RFP. We used our leverage to extend the terms of the deal in a favorable manner for our community. That, too, changed the game.

Lastly, in putting together our presentation, one member of our team asked what turned out to be a very important question: "What is the order of presentations for the seven cities, and how long does each have?" The answer was that we (Tulsa) were last of the seven cities to present, and each city got an hour. That meant the athletic directors and administrators would be in a hotel conference room ALL DAY covering the same information over and over. We anticipated that by the time we got in there, they would be zombies. We had to change the game for them to take notice of our bid.

When we entered the presentation area, in lieu of suits, we were wearing tuxedos and tennis shoes. The four of us who presented came in whooping and hollering and throwing Nerf basketballs all over the room. We got their attention, we had fun with it, and we charged up the audience. We opened our presentation by saying (essentially), "We appreciate the time you have spent in this room all day, and we want to respect that." We used less than half our time, hit the key points, and then had one of our community leaders ask for the sale. He did so by saying, "I'm a volunteer, here to invite you to our city. We are up here in these costumes, which I get is odd, but we wanted to really grab your attention knowing you have been here all day. Costumes or not, one thing I can tell you about the people in Tulsa is that they are VERY good at what they do, and this will be the biggest event in our city when you are there. Thank you for your time, and we'd love to have you in Tulsa. I hope you can use the time we left for a well-deserved break." And we walked out.

The WAC awarded us the tournament for three years when the RFP only had two up for bid. At that time, it was a big deal for our destination. We changed the game, and the WAC leadership responded positively. There are opportunities for people in our industry to change the game every day. Where the opportunity presents itself, let's be like Captain Kirk and create winning scenarios even when one doesn't appear to exist.

Event Bidding Best Practice Spotlight
Nancy Helman, Virginia Beach Sports Marketing

Nancy Helman, Director of Sports Marketing for Virginia Beach, says her organization has a Golden Rule: "Don't write checks with your mouth, that your body can't cash." Virginia Beach Sports Marketing is widely considered one of the top sports commissions in the country. That didn't happen by chance, and as Nancy points out: "If you commit to something during the bidding or negotiation process, you better deliver. Every time. This industry, even with the rapid growth over the past 10 years, is still relatively small and close-knit. Event owners talk to each other. Remember that."

Their record speaks for itself. Virginia Beach Sports Marketing has a client return rate of 86%, which is something critically important to their work. Nancy points out: "That number is really important to us. Our team is dedicated to ensure that every event in Virginia Beach is successful."

One of the things that she says sets the Virginia Beach team apart is its staff make-up. They are all event professionals first and sales people second. "Every member of our team, from top to bottom, started our careers in the event business," Nancy said. "We aren't 'sales people,' we are a team of professionals who know how to locate, bid on, negotiate, and deliver successful events. We know what event owners want because we try to see events through their eyes. In order to create a mutually beneficial relationship, having the ability to create a fiscally-responsible event is necessary, so business decisions need to be made. However, at the end of the day, when the event is wrapped up, we want event owners to say, 'This was my most successful event ever, and if the opportunity presents itself, I am coming back to Virginia Beach because they *get* it.'"

Discussion Questions

1. Host Destinations – Three of the most important things for rights holders when considering a destination are what?

2. Rights Holders – How do the three rights-holder focus areas differ from the key concerns of host cities?

3. Hospitality Leaders – From your perspective, what are the three most important attributes you can contribute to your destination during the bid process?

Stage II
Negotiation and the Home Run Ask

Okay, so we got the event. Now what? In many industries, once the "sale" has been made (in this case the selection of a host site), the work is all but done. In the sports tourism and events space, at this point, we are just now getting started. The real work on an event starts at the negotiating table. Sure, there was a bid, and a formal selection of that bid. However, the final deliverables can only be determined in the contract phase.

Who is to cover added police and security if needed? Who pays for the internet hook-up in the convention center that wasn't clearly outlined in the RFP? If the host cannot deliver enough qualified volunteers, who is responsible to hire, manage, and pay any part-time laborers that are needed? Now, the real work begins.

It is often said that the best contracts are the ones that never have to be reviewed. That is, if you have to dig out an agreement to look at the language in the fine print, there is probably something wrong. While this is likely the truth, it is always important to spend time outlining as many of the specifics you can identify in order to clear up any ambiguity before a problem surfaces.

Our survey work for this project looked at this issue from a different perspective. Rather than try and sort out every possible issue for every sports competition, we wanted to get a feel for the most mission-critical contract elements that host organizations and event organizers encounter every day.

Here are the top three challenges for event rights holders that need to be addressed in the contract phase:

1. Venues – Specifically, damaged venues or venues that are not ready for competition on game day. What are the protocols for rectifying or replacing venues unfit for use?

2. Event support – What are the specific responsibilities of the host entity? What dedicated staff is being offered, and what roles will they play? Also, should the host organization not fulfill on staffing support commitments, what retribution is appropriate to reconcile this issue with the event rights holder?

3. Finances – What financial commitment has been made by the hosting entity, and what specific deliverables are necessary for the event rights holder to capture any incentive dollars that have been allocated? What are the specific deliverables, and when are they due?

From our survey, here are the top three challenges for host communities that need to be considered in the contract phase:

1. RFP consistency – Many times, the contract has in it provisions that are not outlined in the original RFP for the event. In the case where a host community responded to a formal RFP, the contract language should match the terms outlined in the RFP. When there are additions to the contract that were not included in the RFP, all of those items should be negotiable between the parties.

2. Costs – Escalating costs in hosting events was one of the most popular concerns noted by our survey respondents. All financial commitments should be specifically outlined in the contract phase, as well as a contingency clause for items that are not specifically identified in the agreement.

3. Liability – The agreement should specifically outline who is liable for what aspects of the event. Insurance certificates should be issued for each of the involved parties and the contract should hold each entity harmless from one another should a legal issue arise.

As a continuation of Stage I (event bidding) and leading into the contract negotiation phase, we close this section with another case study. This one covers a winning bid scenario, as well as a few negotiation tactics you may be able to use in your next bid process.

Case Study: "Hitting a Home Run"

Many of the articles we have published talk about the importance of an open dialog with your partners. In many instances, the answers they give you can lead you to success. Specific to the sports tourism industry, the insights you gain can be used to craft a winning strategy in bidding to host major events in your communities. Here is one example of how intel obtained from a rights holder helped us land a high-profile championship in Denver.

In 2005, while at the Metro Denver Sports Commission, we were simultaneously building a bid to host the 2008 Frozen Four and a future Women's Final Four. As is often the case, we attended the events as observers each year leading up to our bids. Obviously, anything we could pick up as an onlooker that would differentiate our city would be helpful. Denver is a hotbed for hockey at all levels, so we focused in on landing the Frozen Four.

Throughout the process, we asked the rights holder (the NCAA), past host cities, coaches, players, media,

---

fans, and anyone else who would listen: "What would make this event a home run in Denver?" In the case of the Frozen Four, it became obvious that there were two issues that needed to be addressed.

First, the ice in the host facility had been inconsistent year to year. This was mainly due to the presence of an NHL team in the hosting arenas. The logistics of melting the ice down after an NHL game, repainting the NCAA marks and logos on the ice, and then refreezing the surface, was a tedious one. In order for the ice to be of perfect texture, you had to have people skating on it for days to break it in by the time the Frozen Four teams arrived. This process was often compressed due to the NHL team playing a game in the latest possible window prior to the Frozen Four, and thus, making it hard to get the ice conditioned properly.

The second issue was also related to an NHL tenant. In one of the past host cities of the Frozen Four, there was an NHL team that used the building and it was (to put it nicely) less than hospitable in giving up its arena for the week of the tournament. Numerous people within the collegiate hockey community explained to us how this team had actually gone out of their way to make the Frozen Four staff feel less than welcome. This included not allowing the tournament to use its locker room for one of the collegiate teams.

The NHL team also blocked access to its area of the arena (including NCAA staff, media, the Frozen Four's teams, and ESPN – the tournament's broadcast partner). This was not an ideal situation, and from a community standpoint, the Frozen Four was a big deal, so there was a major disconnect.

As we put together our bid, we realized the two big issues for the NCAA Hockey Committee (that would be deciding the future host sites for the tournament) were really both tied to the NHL team in the venue. We decided to sit down with the leadership of the Colorado Avalanche, who called Denver's Pepsi Center home. We would need their help in alleviating the concerns of an NHL tenant in a Frozen Four building if we were to win the bid for 2008. The President of the Avalanche at that time was Pierre Lacroix. Mr. Lacroix is a legend in hockey and is very well-respected in the sports industry. We explained the issues the NCAA had in another city and asked for his formal support of our bid. At the time, the Avalanche were winning (a lot), and consistently competing for the Stanley Cup (they had won the Cup in 1996 and 2001). Mr. Lacroix not only took a position of support for our effort, but he went one step further – he offered to move the Avalanche out of the building *entirely* should we host the 2008 Frozen Four.

At that time, the first round of the NHL Playoffs was held the same week as the Frozen Four. The NHL Playoffs were best-of-five in round one, so the net effect of Mr. Lacroix's offer was that if the Avalanche were the better seed in the playoffs, they would go on the road in games one and two as the visiting team. In a day when sports were becoming big business, this was a MAJOR commitment on behalf of the Avalanche.

While the ice issue was a big one (we solved that by scheduling youth teams to hold a 24-hour skate on the new ice), the NHL presence was the linchpin. We went into the NCAA bid presentation with a letter from Mr. Lacroix outlining the Avalanche's commitment to embrace the Frozen Four in Denver, and to step aside should we be awarded the event. The members of the NCAA Hockey Committee were floored. Nobody had ever gone to that extent to garner a commitment of that magnitude. We were awarded the event, as well as an NCAA Regional in 2007. The committee thanked us for the level of support we were offering to their championship, and we went to work on creating a truly memorable event.

The 2007 NCAA Western Hockey Regional and the 2008 Frozen Four both set ticket and revenue records for the time. The events were both viewed in our community as smashing successes and established

Denver as a home for major hockey events. Had we not asked the "Home Run" question, I'm not sure we would have had the ammunition to land these prestigious events. While the support of Mr. Lacroix and the Avalanche cannot be overlooked, had we not dug deep into the DNA of the event and its history, we would never have known what to ask our community leaders to support.

Ask your partners what they need. Ask them for the "home run" and then go make it happen to put on the best event your community has ever hosted. Then repeat the cycle again and again and keep hitting home runs.

Negotiation Best Practice Spotlight
Jeff Jarnecke, Former NCAA Executive

Negotiating for something can often times seem awkward. Many people are afraid to ask for something they want if it hasn't been mutually agreed upon in the past. But in all reality, it is often the case that an RFP or bid packet is just the foundation of a much larger discussion. Once an event is secured for a destination, both sides have the right to initiate a discussion about additional elements or ideas that were not part of the initial bid process.

Jeff Jarnecke, former Director of Championships and Alliances at the NCAA, lives in the negotiation world every day. Jarnecke points out: "Negotiations in event solicitation are a MUST and are generally accepted and expected. Bid specifications are usually written in a manner that is heavily weighted, or perhaps even the ideal state, toward the rights holder. While the rights holder would be excited to have a host agree to all the terms as presented, it is uncommon and unlikely. What happens next is contract negotiation, which if done right, can be enjoyable, rewarding, and beneficial for both sides – especially knowing the event could occur some distance in the future. Therefore, a shared understanding at the time of award is of paramount importance."

So, it would seem that all parties in a partnership should leave open the door to negotiate for more amenable terms, or for new things all together. Jarnecke adds: "Rights holders need hosts, and hosts should remember that. Without question, some markets make more sense than others for events, so both the host and rights holder need to identify the following:

1. Non-negotiables.
2. Absolutes.
3. Budget expectations.

Having clear answers on these three elements will aid in the negotiation, as each side will know – and know easily – when it's time to walk away. Meanwhile, the absence of these answers leads to an erosion of quality, logistical challenges, and deficit operations. Having these three questions answered makes the rest of the negotiation reasonable, equitable, and fair, assuming both sides operate in such a manner and place a priority on the other."

"Yes" and "no" are both perfectly acceptable answers, but you cannot get to a yes or no without making the initial ask. No matter what side of the table you are on, it never hurts to raise the question and negotiate.

Discussion Questions

1. Host Destinations – What is the most important question you can ask your event rights holder clients?

2. Rights Holders – If you were to create a best-practice checklist for your potential bid cities to take into account, what would be on it?

3. Hospitality Leaders – Your hotel/restaurant/attraction is hosting a national-level girls soccer tournament. Name three people you could talk to about how to enhance the attendee experience during the event.

Bonus Case Study: "The Art of Negotiation"

"The first principle of contract negotiations is 'Don't remind them of what you did in the past, tell them what you're going to do in the future.'"
– Stan Musial

Business leadership expert Marty Latz once wrote an article outlining the best practices of negotiation. The article was centered on former NBA player-coach-announcer Doug Collins, and it offered some great insights. Collins outlined several tips to negotiation that I believe we can all apply to the sports events industry. Here are three of the tips that Collins offered:

1.   Keep the end goal in mind – Both sides have a desired end result. Each side has a "home run" outcome they want to achieve. Collins advises us to not focus on what other deals look like, but to focus on the win-win outcome for the particular deal you are working on.

2.   Negotiate through truth and trust – This is all about transparency. The more upfront and transparent you are about your position and your goals, the easier it is for the person across the table to trust you and for you to move towards a common ground.

3.   Relationships impact the negotiation process, and as we have discussed in past columns, taking time to build strong relationships can help in all areas of our profession. There is likely no area where this rings true more than in the negotiation process. If you have a foundation to build on through a strong personal or business relationship, you will be able to negotiate in good faith to reach a winning result.

Negotiation is a big part of our everyday lives. It's part of our jobs, our friendships, and our family life. In order to have consistent success, we must become expert negotiators. Collins' thoughts on the end goal, truth and trust, and strong relationships are paramount to finding win-win scenarios in life. I would even add one more – positive thought.

To truly negotiate, we must believe in our hearts that a great outcome will be the end result. We must enter into any negotiation with a positive attitude and a mentality that any barrier can (and will) be overcome. Transparency, trustful relationships, and positive thought. Put those elements in play and championship-level success will be reached.

Stage III
Event Planning and Communication

There is certainly an art to hosting sports competitions. The host communities that deliver the best experience "outside the lines" for their visiting athletes and fans obtain strong favor ratings with event rights holders. Similarly, the event operators and promoters who can make the benchmarks for success clearly understood to those host cities tend to be in high demand for cities to host their championships.

So, what separates the best from the rest? Service. Specifically, superior service of every stakeholder group involved in the event. For the athlete, it's a good competition, at good venues, with an extra touch of caring for their time away from the fields and gym. For the families and fans, it's a safe and clean environment for watching the competition, with some added thought put to activities to explore during their free time. Also, don't forget about the tournament organizers and officials – they too need some special attention, given that they are likely working long shifts over several consecutive days. The best sports organizations, whether they are event owners, host cities, hotels, attractions, or the like, are those that think of the little things and execute with precision.

Specifically, here are three best practices for various

sports tourism and event entities. Plan for these in the lead-up to your events and execute them to offer superior service for your attendees....

Sports Commissions/DMOs

1. Discount Cards for area restaurants and attractions – While this is often done in a haphazard, thrown-together-last-minute manner, we suggest you make this an annual program where you ask the restaurants and attractions to pay a small annual fee to participate for the entire year. You can attach the program to all of your events coming in the next year, which will give you much larger numbers than just trying to offer some discounts for one event over one weekend (for example). During our time at the Phoenix Regional Sports Commission, this program actually became a profit center for us, all while driving traceable ancillary business directly to our local partners. We also used this program as a differentiator during the bid process. Since our program was always running, we could tell our event partners we had it in place right then, so when their event landed in Arizona it would be there for them as well.

2. Event Infrastructure – The top sports commissions have an inventory of event-related equipment that they can move from one venue

to another to support activities "outside the lines" on behalf of their event partners. These items can include coolers, pop-up tents, radios, golf carts, portable scoreboards, or other items relevant to a specific sport you host often. One of our east-coast clients actually owns its own timing system for use in its events, and for rental to local community groups and their 5K fundraisers. The opportunity here is to use these items to support your bid-in or created events, and also help drive rental revenues back to the organization through community user groups that need them for their tournaments and events.

3. Supporting Event Staff – Industry expert, Josh Todd, offers up the following advice: "For our area of the country (Mesa, AZ) it was always, 'Do we have more than enough water?' Donated, purchased, bottles, coolers – there should be so much that there is enough left over for your next event. Then, nothing short of a family emergency should take priority during the event execution."

Local Organizing Committee (LOC)

1. Staging Vehicles – If your event happens to include complimentary vehicles for coaches, officials, or VIPs, map out a staging plan where those vehicles are all at the host hotel. Meet the

VIPs at the airport, hand them an envelope with their hotel key and room number (pre-check-in, of course), along with their car keys, vehicle type, and where the vehicle is parked at the hotel. Then, escort them to baggage claim for their bags (if they checked any) and direct them to the hotel shuttle or Uber transport you have ready for them. Being in a new city, this is a stress-free trip for them to their assigned hotel where they can go straight to their room and go identify their car when ready. They don't have to go through any checkout lines or try and navigate a new city after a long day of travel. Post-event, you can put a team together to gather the keys at the hotel sites and return the cars to the proper locations (rental agency or dealership). During our work in Denver, this was one of the most popular programs we had for the coaches, officials, and conference leaders for our collegiate events.

2. Official/Coach Hospitality – Provide an area at the primary venue, and also at the host hotel, for coaches and officials to rest and relax. We suggest comfortable sitting areas and an offering of water and snacks throughout the day. As an extra benefit, we suggest offering up late-night meals for officials in the hotel hospitality room, as they likely will be working games into the evening when most limited service properties may not have room service.

3. Staff Support – Every event needs at least one person dedicated to handling external challenges that may arise. In Phoenix, we had Ed. Ed was Ed Durkin, and Ed loved to execute events. He was on hand for all of our major events, and he had a rule of thumb: "Anything less than $300 that needed fixing, fix it." We would deal with the fallout after the event. His job was to make sure our event partners could focus on their competition ("inside the lines") and Ed would handle any issues "outside the lines." Ed provided handwarmers to officials during a frost delay, he picked up VIPs at the airport who were flying in last minute and he replenished coffee and snacks when they ran out. He did it all. Funny thing about Ed was that he wasn't our event manager – he was our lead marketing staff member. He just liked events, and he was *good* at it. Every event, big or small, we didn't hesitate to put Ed on the front lines. Our event partners came to love working with us largely due to the great service they had received from just one person: Ed. A small commitment on our part, a big return in happy customers, and renewed events for the future.

Host Hotel

1. The Ante – To be considered an average host hotel for even the smallest of championships,

you need to provide the basics: team pre-check-in to avoid lines, free WiFi, inclusive breakfast, free parking, a no smoking environment, satellite TV, an information table about area attractions (usually staffed by a CVB volunteer), and ample F&B options in the hotel or nearby. These are the "Ante" to play in this space. If you don't have them, a good game plan to fulfill client requests in these areas would be a great tactic (example: if you have no F&B on site, offer to pre-order pizza and salads from an area Italian restaurant for the teams playing late games that night, so when they get back to the hotel, the food is ready for them). Find ways to work around deficiencies to make sure you meet the threshold of service your visitors are seeking.

2. Arrival – Little things go a long way in your guest-first impression. Examples: having your frontline staff in event t-shirts or referee shirts at check-in, using a GOBO light to illuminate the event logo on the lobby floor for athletes to see when they arrive, posting a bracket board and event schedule each day (while the tournament world has largely gone electronic, the athletes always love to see their team name up on the board, and the fact that your staff will take the time to update the board will mean more to the athletes than looking at their phone app).

3. Value Ads – Beyond the Ante, there are numerous ways you can make the lives of your visiting teams more enjoyable. Here are five of the best: (1) a coach and team-manger hospitality room, kept open late and stocked with drinks and light food options/snacks, (2) a team room set up with video games, snacks, a ping pong table, and other relaxing activities for non-game times, (3) a laundry room with multiple washers and dryers, including free detergent, (4) an athlete training area (could be in the team room) with a trainer table to tape ankles or get ice treatment. Include in this room a dedicated ice machine (small pellets preferred) as well as a supply of ice bags and ankle tape that will last the entire event. This last item is as important to your non-tournament guests as it is to your visiting athletes (ever had a floor run out of ice due to athletes using the machines to fill their ice bags?).

Case Study: "Teamwork through Communication"

"The single biggest problem in communication is the illusion that it has taken place."
– George Bernard Shaw

During the 2014 NFL season, Peyton Manning led the Denver Broncos to the Super Bowl in New York. In the weeks leading up to the big game, much was being made about Manning's signal call of "Omaha! Omaha!" Manning's high level of communication is legendary. This advanced level of communication is not only necessary to run a complicated NFL offense, but is every bit as important to sports industry professionals in leading our organizations. As an avid football fan (and the son of a football coach), I'm still no expert on the nuances of running an offense. However, I think we can all gain insights from watching an elite quarterback run his business and apply those to our daily lives. Here are four communication skills that we can steal from Peyton Manning:

1.   Be clear – At the line of scrimmage, Manning's voice is discernable and forceful. He balances the play calls with hand signals to make sure everyone is on the same page before the snap. Even after he has called a play, he is still talking to his teammates to make sure they know where to be and what is coming next. His message is easily understood, which limits mistakes by teammates.

2.   Be concise – Great leaders are very specific about the results they are looking to achieve. Those

that make their goals transparent and communicate them effectively to their followers are more apt to achieve success.

3.   Be direct – There is little wasted time or energy in calling a play and getting the ball snapped. You only have 40 seconds on the play clock, so there is little time to waste. In our communications with our work teams, cut through the clutter and get right to the point. Time is a valuable asset. Cut to the chase and make the most of it.

4.   Be prompt – Communication needs to be delivered in a timely fashion for someone to utilize the information. If someone is waiting on information to keep a project moving ahead, the chances of success diminish with each passing moment. A great goal is to try to never have anyone waiting on you. Get out in front of projects and stay there.

Even though the Broncos' Super Bowl run fell short that year, much can be learned from the combatants. The coaches and the quarterbacks are technically the CEOs of their teams. The team that communicates their game plan in the most effective manner usually wins the Lombardi Trophy. We all have our personal goals – our own Super Bowls to win. Learn from the best, in sports and in life, put their examples to work, and hoist that trophy.

Discussion Questions

1. Host Destinations – How many stakeholder groups do you need to communicate with leading up to, and during, an event? List them.

2. Rights Holders – List three best practices you can employ to keep your event team (LOC, host community, staff, volunteers, etc.) up to date on the pre-event planning as it progresses.

3. Hospitality Leaders – Who do you need information from in order to best service your visitors/clients during the event? How do you plan to communicate with them prior to, and during, the event? If you are a hotel, what items would you add to the "Value Ads" list?

Stage IV
Pre-Game

While we have already covered event planning and communication, the following "Pre-Game" section is focused on that time just before launch. Consider this similar to the countdown when NASA sends a rocket into orbit. 10. 9. 8. 7. 6.... You get the idea.

In this window of time, we want to really lock down the critical-path elements of the event, and make sure all deliverables are met and that we are ready to get the event started down the right path.

To best articulate the crucial nature of this time in the event-planning process, we are offering up this subject's best practice spotlight up front, right here at the beginning of this chapter. We hope this can frame up the discussion....

Pre-Game Planning Best Practice Spotlight
Jeff Golner, Agency G, Fiesta Bowl Committee Past Chairman

For many destinations, college bowl games offer a significant exposure opportunity, as well as a tourism bounce in the winter months. Our home state of Arizona is no different. Arizona is host to three bowl games annually, and in most years a fourth game in the form of a college football playoff game.

The Fiesta Bowl Committee is the major driver of our college-bowl-game engine, with over 300 key community leaders volunteering their time and resources to support their two games annually (the Fiesta Bowl and the Cheez-It Bowl, formerly known as the Cactus Bowl). One of the Fiesta Bowl's long-time leaders, both on the field and off, is Jeff Golner, the founder and owner of sports marketing company Agency G.

Jeff has literally been working the sidelines of these bowl games for over a decade, and he served as the Fiesta Bowl's Committee Chairman in 2017-2018. He also is the proud owner of a World Series ring, having served as the on-field event coordinator for the Arizona Diamondbacks when they claimed the title in 2001. Jeff has produced hundreds of events, from the early concept phases to final execution. We asked him what the most important elements of event planning are as game day approaches. Here are his comments:

"Even in advance of College Football's Selection Sunday, the Fiesta Bowl office will have communicated with all eligible teams that may come to Arizona for either the Cheez-It or Fiesta Bowls. Forms and surveys are advanced, and a good info dump will already have been performed. Teams also know that either the Tuesday or Wednesday following Selection Sunday are set up as site-visit days. These site visits include, at a minimum, tours of the team hotel, practice site, and stadium. From those dates, the bowl games are now anywhere from 21 to 27 days out, so getting ahead of operational and logistical-borne tasks is essential."

Golner continues: "Additionally, at the site visit, manuals are distributed to all key football stakeholders, including the Director of Football Operations and Media Operations personnel. Information is also readily available for team bands, cheer and pom squads, and certainly alumni staffers."

More from Jeff: "Shortly after the team-personnel site visit, assigned volunteer committee members, specifically team liaisons, along with a Fiesta Bowl staff and board member, make a visit to each school's campus. This helps bridge the gap and to show the Bowl's unmatched hospitality efforts. This crew hosts the on-campus student-athlete's gift suite experience and serves as another touch point to align ourselves with the football operations staff, as well as the student-athletes. At the end of the day, and for that matter, the entire Bowl experience, the Fiesta Bowl does everything possible to see-through a memory making event, regardless of the outcome of the big game."

That is a lot to take in. Note the number of non-athletes that are under consideration here. The moral of the story is, communicate to all of your event stakeholders for success.

So, you may say, "We are never going to be that big, or be on ESPN, or have the kind of resources some of those big events have." In that case, you are probably right. However, no matter the size of your event, your destination, or your organization, we all need to provide our partners, guests, and visitors with a level of executional commitment that makes them want to work with us again in the future. Oftentimes, making an event a memorable one involves the use of volunteers (FYI, the Fiesta Bowl's driving force isn't their staff, it's the 300-plus business leaders in the community that do a great deal of the heavy lifting).

With the importance of sustainable volunteerism in mind, we introduce this chapter's case study....

Case Study: Volunteer Management
"The Virtual Bench"

Late summer in our home state of Arizona brings with it monsoon season. Every afternoon the clouds roll in and Mother Nature takes over. While these storms are quite turbulent, they are normally harmless beyond a few lightning bolts and a strong downpour of rain in a short window of time. However, one storm created an issue for our family. When the storm hit, we were at our church, just down the street from our house. When we walk to church each week, we use the electric garage door to get in and out of

---

our house. The storm knocked out power in the neighborhood and made our garage door inoperable. We didn't have any keys with us, so we couldn't get back into the house after church. The power was out for more than 90 minutes, so we were completely isolated from the world for that time (no cell phones, no computers, no TV, no wallets or access to a car). The moral of the story is to have a back-up plan.

In the business world, we need to have alternative plans when things don't work out the way we had predicted. Nowhere is this more important than in building our work teams. As we accumulate talented team members, over time they will have additional opportunities. This is especially true of non-profit sports organizations or DMOs that often hire young (affordable) talent. Eventually, they will build their skills and be recruited by others to move to a new position elsewhere. In these cases, we need a back-up plan. We need a virtual bench.

The concept of the virtual bench is to continuously recruit talent. You may not have a staff vacancy today, but at some point, you will, so we need to constantly be on the lookout for the next key acquisition. The virtual bench represents the people that you would go to if a staffing (or volunteer) need arises. Ask yourself, if your top sales person left tomorrow morning, who would you call? What about your lead event services manager? What if your committee chair had to step down a month before your event? If they left, do you know who you would recruit to fill the hole? We recommend that you ask this question of everyone on your team, both volunteers and staff, and even about yourself. If you left, what is the game plan? If there isn't one, and you want your legacy to survive your departure, help build the succession plan for the organization.

In order to build a sustainable organization, we need to continually fill the pipeline with talent. Talented staff, talented volunteers, talented partners, talented everything. We always need to build our virtual benches and be ready to leap into action when a need arises. Think of it as if you are an athletic director and your head football coach suddenly leaves for another school. Do you have a list of candidates in the top desk drawer ready to go? As leaders, we should always be ready for change.

Singer Gwen Stefani once said, "Let's be realistic, it's not going to be like this forever" (editor's note: Stefani was quoted as saying this before her role in the TV show "The Voice"). Take time to actively cultivate your virtual bench. The more time and resources you spend on this process now, the better position you will be in when change comes in the future.

With volunteerism and pre-game planning in mind, as we approach event launch, here are three things we take away from Jeff Golner's comments:

1. Host Destinations – Over-communicate verbally and in writing. To teams, fans, local businesses, community leaders, elected officials, to everyone. If you think someone or some group may be a stakeholder in an event's success, they are. Build an inclusive communication plan and execute it vigorously.

2. Rights Holders – Even if you are not as big of an organization as the Fiesta Bowl, you can plan out key touch points to make sure your guests know you are thinking of them prior to game day. Do your fans know that a particular destination is famous for music, food, amusement parks, etc., and how to access that when the competition isn't taking place? Do the athletes' families know that the hotels are offering late checkouts on race day since the marathon won't finish until after noon local time? Don't depend on the host to do all the communicating. Map out a game plan and try to touch all parties with relevant and VIP-level information.

3. Hospitality Leaders – Team liaisons are important in the pre-game phase to serve as

connection points for your soon-to-be visitors. Assign them to the visiting teams and their leadership early and let them serve as a resource to those teams in advance, and during, their visit. Some teams may not want to lean on these liaisons, and that is okay, because it's our responsibility as hosts to at least provide relevant resources to our guests. (Note: The NAIA excels at the team liaison concept and has even managed ways to monetize the program through nominal local sponsorships).

This entire chapter may seem rudimentary, mundane, and second nature to many. It also could appear to be tedious, and a little too overreaching. At the end of the day, our industry is about partnerships. Partners that are long-term, and are built on trust, and communication. There is likely no more important characteristic in a partnership than being able to trust in the people on the other side – that they will communicate, and that they will do what they say they are going to do. This is most important right before launch, and of course, on game day.

Discussion Questions

1. Host Destinations – If you were to build a communication playbook, what facts about your community would you include? As an exercise, list 8-10 of those items now.

2. Rights Holders – Who is on your virtual bench?
List the top three staff and volunteer positions
related to your organization or department.
Now write down one person for each position
that can be part of your virtual bench. How can
you continue to cultivate relationships with
those individuals?

3. Hospitality Leaders – Name five critical items
for an upcoming event that you need to have on
hand to communicate to your work teams.
Who has the answers to those items and how
will you obtain them?

Stage V
Game Day

There is an old saying in golf: "All bets are won on the first tee." What that means in English is that the framework for success is in place well in advance of the game being played. The way *Sports Service* is laid out, we are trying to set the stage for a memorable event through a great planning process.

Now that game day is here, what are the best practices to deliver on the elements that have been negotiated, as well as those "home run" stretch goals we talked about in Stage II? Below, we offer three game-day best practices for each of the three stakeholder groups we have outlined in this book.

Host Destinations

1. Special Events – Industry expert Josh Todd (Disney, Mesa Sports, Connect Sports, and currently President and Executive Director of the Omaha Sports Commission) offers up a way to make a tournament a memory: "Little things make events memorable, and memorable events usually come back to that host city. One thing we did at Disney, which I took with me and have used in other events, was honoring kids' birthdays. It's a simple idea and easily pulled from planners' registrations. If a youth athlete has a birthday during the event, bring a card and

a little gift to them at their game. This goes a long way, and the reactions are always priceless!"

2. Destination DNA – Nancy Helman of Virginia Beach Sports Marketing offers up a way to separate your community from the pack: "In Virginia Beach, we play up to our best asset… the Beach. We know that in Virginia Beach, athletes, coaches, families, and fans can combine their competition and vacation to provide an "added value" experience. Oftentimes, for our larger events, our Visitor Information Center will set up a satellite location at event registration or during the busiest times of the competition to help guests with directions, make restaurant recommendations, and give them suggestions on how to make the most of their stay in our City." The moral of the story is to use your destination's uniqueness to create a memory in a way that other communities cannot.

3. The Client – The event rights holder is your client, and in nearly all cases, their staff will be working very long hours consecutively for several days to execute a great event. Ask the leader of the event team what you can do for their staff to make their time during the event better. The host can offer up late-night meals

hot-and-ready at the host hotel each night of competition, a "thank you" reception or dinner the last night after the event is over, or early morning customized delivery of their favorite coffee.

Rights Holders

1. Communication – Messaging what the game-day success looks like is critical. Does everyone involved in the event know their role and what the goals are from one day to the next? We recommend early-morning "stand up" meetings each day to keep everyone on the same page. These meetings should be brief (15 minutes max) and focus on that particular day's schedule, any logistical challenges that may lie ahead, and what the major goals are for the day.

2. Volunteer Engagement – Personally thank your key volunteers. That will not only help you in getting the best out of them, but it will also help your hosting organization retain their volunteers over the long run. Happy volunteers make for a great event environment.

3. Host Partners – Make it a point each day of your event to reach out to your primary contact for the host destination. Make sure they are getting what they want out of the partnership each day and ask them what you can do to make

their day a positive one. We know this is hard to do in the midst of executing an event, but a little check-in with your hosts will go a long way towards a successful championship.

Hospitality Leaders

1. Event Enhancement – GOBO lights in the lobby (or at the entrance at an attraction or restaurant) with the event logo offer a welcoming environment for the participating teams and their families. It's a small thing but makes a big impact.

2. Community Engagement – Invite key stakeholders to the event. The more they can see and experience when an event is in town, the better the understanding they will have for the impact of sports tourism on your community and your business.

3. Amenities – Leaving a special welcome gift in the room of the team's travel planner and the head coach upon arrival will make them feel welcome in your community – another small thing that can be the start to a renewal for the following year.

Game Day Best Practice Spotlight
Beth Porreca, USA Football, Director of Events

Beth Porreca is one of the most well-respected event professionals in our industry. She has been leading event teams and producing national and international events for over 15 years. Her work at Disney Sports, US Lacrosse, and now USA Football has garnered Beth numerous awards and recognitions for her work specific to event planning and execution.

While this section is about game day, we thought at this point, it would be good to insert thoughts from Beth on the event *process*. We asked her three questions on her views in this area and add one story she shared with us a few years ago....

Question: What variables go into your site selection process?
Answer (Beth): The most important thing is always the venue and making sure it's a best-in-class facility with the appropriate infrastructure for an event. For example, if you know that weather might be an issue, having all-weather fields and lights for evening play is a key decision factor. Additionally, the facility infrastructure is important, and having on-site restrooms and concession stands is a huge cost savings to event owners who would otherwise have to provide those amenities through a third party, which adds to the overall expense budget. Additional factors

include ease of travel to the area, hotel room availability and rates, and destination activities that meet the needs of your event demographic.

Q: What can a destination do to make sure they DO NOT get your business?

A: The venue or facility staff and their ability to mesh with our event staff, specifically the event lead, is important. If we find a fantastic venue, but the staff is unwilling to listen to our team or work with us, then we will most likely go somewhere else more accommodating. As an event owner, the facility becomes a reflection of your brand, and the facility staff becomes brand ambassadors. If they can't fulfill that role, then we won't take an event to them.

Q: What is your most important advice to event planners on game day?

A: The key to successful game-day execution is no different for an event planner than it is for a high-level athlete. Focus on the fundamentals and stick to your game plan.... No matter what happens – and this is the key – stay calm. As an event planner, you are the leader of your team and your attitude and actions dictate the attitude and actions on not only those surrounding you at any given moment, but also of your staff and your volunteers. If you are frantic, everyone is frantic. As one of my colleagues always says, "Be a duck: no matter how hard you are swimming under water, on the surface, project a calm demeanor."

Within Beth's comments (as is the case with most event planners) there is obviously a lean towards good facilities and positive working relationships. One example of something that worked for us in Phoenix when we worked with Beth and US Lacrosse is outlined on page 26. We had Ed. The moral to that story is that the best host communities make sure their event rights holder partners (like Beth) can focus on the execution of their events and nothing more. The best hosts put in place a support system to allow the rights holder to put on a superior competition on the field, while the host makes sure the attendees garner a superior experience off the field.

Case Study: Game Day
"Lemons into Lemonade, Sports Event Awesome"

One of my favorite public speakers is a Canadian author-blogger-tweeter named Scott Stratten. Scott has an unwavering dedication to tell stories of business "Awesome." He spreads the gospel where people across the world take work situations that look like lemons and turn them into lemonade. Below is a personal story from my experiences in running

---

sporting events. We can call this a case study for "Sports Events Awesome" (trademark pending, unless Scott already has it).

In 2001, I was fortunate to be the event director of the Western Athletic Conference Basketball tournament in Tulsa, Oklahoma. The WAC, as it is known, was a great league back then. Some of the legends of college basketball coached in the league (including Jerry Tarkanian, Billy Tubbs, and Don Haskins) and the level of play was elite, even on the worst nights. However, one small conversation that week in Tulsa forever shaped how I look at opportunities to enrich an event, and it had nothing to do with the basketball court. During the event we had our official travel agency housed within the arena. They had their own in-house television feed of the games going on in the building, and as teams appeared to be poised to get knocked out of the tournament, the travel agents started booking outbound flights for them. At the time, Tulsa's airport didn't offer many opportunities to get 20-30 people out of town on a moment's notice, so the travel agents were busy trying to find options quickly as teams were eliminated (the Tulsa airport is *much* better and bigger now, FYI). As you can guess, when teams get knocked out of a tournament, coaches often don't want to hang around town when they have lost – they can be cranky like that. So, our goal was to get them home as quickly as we could upon elimination.

The travel agency was also responsible for getting bands and cheerleaders out of town when their basketball teams lost, as well. This is where the AWESOME occurred.... The University of Texas at El Paso (UTEP) lost a close game in the semifinals late Friday night. The travel agency got the basketball team on a plane early Saturday morning to head home, but there were no seats available to get the band back to Texas. The band had flights booked for Sunday, and now they were going to have to stay in Tulsa for two more days. A call came over the radio for me to report to the travel office. I assumed that a coach was waiting for me to express the team's displeasure about not getting an immediate flight out of town, but when I arrived in the office, it was a completely different conversation that awaited me. The band director for UTEP was there, and I was brought up to speed on their plight (having to stay in Tulsa two more nights). The band director, however, had asked for me to come talk to him not because he was upset, but because he wanted to be Awesome.

One of the member schools in the WAC back then was the University of Hawaii. Hawaii had defeated UTEP on that Friday night. Due to the high costs of housing and travel, Hawaii rarely had their band travel with them to the mainland for road games. UTEP's band director noticed this and posed a question to me: "Hawaii didn't bring their band, did they?" I confirmed that they hadn't.

He then said, "Well, we are here until Sunday. Can we play for them in the championship game tomorrow night?"

I wasn't sure I understood what he was saying, as I had NEVER heard of a rival school's band supporting another team. So, after he clarified that they would like to literally play FOR Hawaii, I looked around the room and said, "Why not?"

On my way to the arena that Saturday night, I did have concerns about what they would be wearing, and how they would actually represent Hawaii. As soon as I walked in, those concerns calmed immediately.

The UTEP band took their place in the north end of the arena (Hawaii's designated section), with a national television audience tuning in on ESPN. In seats that would likely have been empty, they filled in the section for Hawaii's band and really added to the atmosphere of the event.

The band director (being Awesome on his own volition), had gone to Wal-Mart that day and bought 20 reasonably-priced Hawaiian button-down shirts in pastel colors. He also scored some flower necklaces that played the part of the Hawaiian lei. So, come game time (and ESPN time) they looked the part. And, the topper of it all, when the Hawaii team came running out of the tunnel to take the court, the band keyed up and played the TV theme song to Hawaii Five-O (Dah-dahnana-nah-na, dah-dahnana- na....).

As I went over to thank the UTEP band's director (in near tears, I might add), I said, "I have to ask. How did you think of the Five-O song?" He said they were happy to participate in the championship game and commented about their musical selection: "We don't know their fight song, so it's the closest thing we had." I said, "AWESOME."

This is a great example of how to take a negative event and turn it into a win-win outcome for all involved. The band had a good time, the arena had an improved atmosphere, and I'm sure the Hawaii team appreciated the added support. The practice of bands playing for competing schools has since become a tradition in the WAC. It all started with one band leader looking at a situation in a very different way.

We all have opportunities for "Sports Event Awesome." Let's make sure when the moment arrives, we are ready to take advantage of them!

Discussion Questions

1. Host Destinations – Give three examples of how the host destination can stand out from the competition.

2. Rights Holders – Outline two ways that a rights holder can enhance their communications during an event.

3. Hospitality Leaders – List three things a host hotel or attraction can employ to make the teams, coaches and fans feel welcome when they arrive in your community.

Stage VI
Post-Game

One of the most important tasks to tend to after the event concludes is scheduling and executing a post-con, or post-conference meeting. In today's world, where everyone is trying to do more with less and we are all busy, this is often overlooked.

Omaha's Josh Todd adds this: "It really doesn't matter if the post-con is in-person or on the phone – rather, just that it happens as soon as possible after the event when everything is fresh in your mind."

If you believe that post-cons are just one more thing you don't have time for, think of it in this perspective......

The post-con is the first sales call for the renewal of the event.

Don't take that opportunity for granted.

Discussion Question

1. When is it okay to bypass the post-con meeting?

Stage VII
Renew and Repeat!

In order to sustain success, you really need a clear
vision and an understanding of how your organization
defines "victory." Without that understanding, you
will always question if your organization is really
meeting the end goal. Once you clearly understand
how success is defined, you will have the gratification
of knowing, without question, when you have
achieved it. Getting there is one thing but staying
there is another.

It takes great leadership and focus to sustain a high-
level of success over the long haul. In my experience,
all great leaders are great communicators and
motivators. They are not afraid to surround
themselves with the best talent in the industry.
Organizational success may start with the leader, and
many times that person gets the public credit, but it is
always the collective efforts of the total team that
drives sustained success.

In order to renew and repeat, you have to prospect
the right clients and secure the right partnerships from
the beginning. If you don't do these things then it's
likely going to be a one-and-done deal, and in the long
term, that benefits no one. Know your organization's
capabilities, what you do well, and more importantly,
what you don't. Build your partnerships with a clear
understanding of both. In the event business, things

go wrong. And when they do, you need to act swiftly with suggestions for a fix or work around and be transparent with all of your partners. This is not easy to do, but it's a must if you want to build long-lasting partnerships.

In a nut shell, you have to have a clear vision, strong leadership, consistent communications, the right clients and partnerships, be transparent, under-promise, and always over-deliver. If your organization can activate on the above items, you will achieve organizational success, and you will most definitely be able to renew business and thus, repeat success. This will give your organization a foundation for growth to capture a larger market share and more business over the long term.

Final Discussion Questions

1. List your three biggest takeaways from *Sports Service*.

2. What area(s) of servicing sports groups would you like to know more about that this book didn't cover? (Please email your thoughts on this topic to Jon@HuddleUpGroup.com).

Acknowledgments

This book would not have been possible without the enormous amount of feedback we received from leaders in the sports tourism and events industry.

Our sincerest "thanks" go out to the professionals who contributed to this book and who make our industry such a great place to work each and every day:

Glen Schorr, Willy Leparulo, Phillip Wright, Joe Pickett, Mark Koski, Beth Porreca, Jeff Jarnecke, Brent Paulson, Stacey Hepp, Phil Andrews, Jennifer Miles, Erika Conklin, Marion Wohlrab, Brian D'Amico, Rick Long, Pete Bryden, Scott Wollaston, Matthew Payne, Kindra Fry, Matt Ten Haken, Gregg Cook, Mark Rath, and Josh Todd.

Special thanks to our own Jordan Parry for all his time in editing the book over and over again.

Also, a shout out to Huddle Up Group team member, Caroline Brown, for her help designing the cover.